HAL•LEONARD INSTRUMENTAL PLAY-ALONG

TENOR SAX

AUDIO ACCESS INCLUDED

PLAYBACK+
Speed • Pitch • Balance • Loop

PEACEFUL HYMNS

Audio arrangements by Peter Deneff

To access audio visit:
www.halleonard.com/mylibrary

Enter Code
1708-7774-9677-0418

ISBN 978-1-70513-792-5

HAL•LEONARD®

Visit Hal Leonard Online at
www.halleonard.com

Contact us:
Hal Leonard
7777 West Bluemound Road
Milwaukee, WI 53213
Email: info@halleonard.com

In Europe, contact:
Hal Leonard Europe Limited
42 Wigmore Street
Marylebone, London, W1U 2RN
Email: info@halleonardeurope.com

In Australia, contact:
Hal Leonard Australia Pty. Ltd.
4 Lentara Court
Cheltenham, Victoria, 3192 Australia
Email: info@halleonard.com.au

ABIDE WITH ME

TENOR SAX

Music by WILLIAM H. MONK

ALL CREATURES OF OUR GOD AND KING

TENOR SAX

Music from *Geistliche Kirchengesang*

ALL HAIL THE POWER OF JESUS' NAME

TENOR SAX

Music by OLIVER HOLDEN

ALL THROUGH THE NIGHT

TENOR SAX

Welsh Folksong

AMAZING GRACE

TENOR SAX

Traditional American Melody

BE THOU MY VISION

TENOR SAX

Traditional Irish

BLESSED ASSURANCE

TENOR SAX

Music by PHOEBE PALMER KNAPP

COME, THOU FOUNT OF EVERY BLESSING

TENOR SAX

Music from John Wyeth's *Repository of Sacred Music*

FAIREST LORD JESUS

TENOR SAX

Music from *Schlesische Volkslieder*

FOR THE BEAUTY OF THE EARTH

TENOR SAX

Music by CONRAD KOCHER

GREAT IS THY FAITHFULNESS

TENOR SAX

Music by WILLIAM M. RUNYAN

HOLY, HOLY, HOLY

TENOR SAX

Music by JOHN B. DYKES

HOW FIRM A FOUNDATION

TENOR SAX

Traditional music compiled by JOSEPH FUNK

I NEED THEE EVERY HOUR

TENOR SAX

Music by ROBERT LOWRY

IT IS WELL WITH MY SOUL

TENOR SAX

Music by PHILIP P. BLISS

JUST AS I AM

TENOR SAX

Music by WILLIAM B. BRADBURY

THE KING OF LOVE MY SHEPHERD IS

TENOR SAX

Traditional Irish Melody

LET ALL MORTAL FLESH KEEP SILENCE

TENOR SAX

17th Century French Carol

MY FAITH LOOKS UP TO THEE

TENOR SAX

Music by LOWELL MASON

NEARER, MY GOD, TO THEE

TENOR SAX

Music by LOWELL MASON

WERE YOU THERE WHEN THEY CRUCIFIED MY LORD?

TENOR SAX

Traditional

WHAT A FRIEND WE HAVE IN JESUS

TENOR SAX

Music by CHARLES C. CONVERSE

WONDROUS LOVE

TENOR SAX

Southern American Folk Hymn